A NOTE FROM KELLY...

Dear New Friend,

I can't... I won't... God will never... It's impossible... I don't have enough... Everyone is treating me... I am no good... I can't believe I... I am so....

For a long time, this is how I talked to myself. I believed I was stuck, useless and was never going to amount to much. I believed God helped others, but not me. He had better things to do.

Do you struggle this way? No doubt life, at times, is a hard-fought battle. I know how it is...

I've battled: an eating disorder, depression, fear, doubts, anger, worry, a health crisis that threatened to leave me unable to walk, financial issues and relational problems. I know battle well.

I also know what it is to live in an endless cycle of doubt, fear and discouragement...in a pit that feels impossible to climb out of. Is that where you live?

You know what else I discovered? I saw that through God's truth, promises and wisdom, there is an escape. I found it.

I discovered there are 12 focus areas in life that could change my mind, and then my life. I implemented them and wrote about how you can too in my book, Battle Ready: Train your Mind to Conquer Challenges, Defeat Doubt and Live Victoriously. It is easy to change when you have a plan.

This prayer journal is about helping you put practical wisdom into action. It is also about helping you discover your vision and your mission through prayer, so you live a life that matters.

I assure you, God has your every answer.

My hope is that this book blesses you.

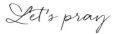

Father God, you are the ultimate change-maker. You are Healer. You are Restorer. You are Maker and Creator of all new things. I ask for your help for every reader as she begins to train her mind to conquer challenges and defeat doubt. I ask you to help her put in action the portions of the book that will most help her in her journey. I ask you to make clear what she should do in her life. I ask you to encourage her along the way. May all of this be done for your glory and honor. In Jesus' Name. Amen.

KELLY BALARIE

www.purposefulfaith.com
Author, Fear Fighting & Battle Ready
Twitter/Instagram: @kellybalarie

Copyright © 2018 Kelly Balarie. All Rights Reserved.

HOW TO USE THE BATTLE READY DAILY PRAYER JOURNAL

This journal is designed to help you transform your mind, so you can transform your life through God's Word. This book is designed to breed confidence and go-power. It is prepared in a way to help you learn and see through what you might normally forget to do. If you focus on the daily and just do it, before you know it, you will have done it. That's the idea behind this journal.

THERE ARE 5 MAIN SECTIONS. LET ME EXPLAIN EACH OF THEM:

1. THE 3 BIG ETERNITY GOALS:

Uncover the big visions for your life. Through prayer, you will discover what is "most important" for you to focus on, so you're not constantly driven by "the unimportant". Some of my BIG Eternity Goals are: Creating a Whole-Hearted Loving Family, Setting People Free and Loving People and God Intensely. These are the things I want to be "known for" when I die. You'll ask God and discover your own big things. As you pray through the days, they will likely evolve. (Other examples: love my son well, become a counselor to love others, be a large financial giver, adopt and bring up a loving wise child)

2. WHAT TO DO TODAY:

This is where you ask God, "What do I practically need to do to see these BIG eternity goals through?" The answers can be either practical or more focused on changing a mind-habit. Changing a mind-habit or perspective is just as important as doing something tangible, such as: filling out paperwork to adopt the child, or making that call. Don't be fooled by hands-on doing. Clearing out the mentalities that keep you stuck is just as important. As you know, there are nearly a bazillion ideas in the Battle Ready book to hone in on. You certainly want to consider the 12 focus areas as you begin to change your life. Also consider the question, "God, who do you want me to love today?"

Some of these to-dos will repeat day to day, while others may remain for 66+ days. If you fail to see them through, that's okay. Don't give up.

Copyright © 2018 Kelly Balarie. All Rights Reserved.

3. GETTING NEGATIVITY & MISTRUTHS OUTTA THE WAY:

Think back to when you attempted to tackle something like this before. What stopped you from doing so? What negative thoughts, doubts or fears came to throw you off track? Be specific with them. Write them down exactly as they hit your mind. Then, refute them with truth, with God's Word, with prayer and with a new script, so you are prepared and armed-up for your day.

Keep in Mind:

1. It takes 66 days to form a new habit.

2. This DOES NOT mean you won't fail some along the way.

3. All warriors fall down at times, but they always get back up again.

4. If you forget to pray some days, the journal still waits for you. Grace abounds!

5. Talk to yourself kindly, like you would to a good friend.

Once the lies are removed, replace them with the truth. You want to create a new thought to overpower the old one. For example, exchange "I can't" for "With Christ, all things are possible."

Make a plan to think well.

4. NOW I PRAY:

Here, you want to pray, listen and write down God's heart for you after prayer. Note encouragement, conviction, a sense of what He might do, the depths of His love, insights or wisdom that comes.

My sheep hear my voice, and I know them, and they follow me. (Jo. 10:27)

But seek first his kingdom and his righteousness, and all these things will be given to you as well. (Mt. 6:33)

5. TRUST GOD ALONG THE WAY:

Write down what God might teach or provide you, how He'll grow you, and how relationships will change. Take an inventory of how you will feel as a result of these actions and reflections.

Be inspired by the scripture and Battle Ready quotes at the top of each page. You can also use the free pages in the back, for any extra journal notes you may have.

Copyright © 2018 Kelly Balarie. All Rights Reserved.

QUICK TIPS:

one

Don't prioritize the urgent over your important.
Life will rule you, instead of you trusting God's rule over it.

Two

Avoid distractions when you go through this journal.
Turn off your phone, your computer and TV.

Three

Choose to recreate the tedious things you must do. Consider ways to bring
God into them. Example: sing when doing the dishes, recite one of these
Bible verses when doing laundry, or pray when driving in the car.

four

Consider how to reduce life stressors. First, acknowledge what they are.
Then, figure out if you can stop doing them, delegate to someone else
or look at them in a new way.

five

Let love prevail. If love never fails, then love is always a good starting and
ending point. Brick by brick, construct a life that matters - and lasts.

six

Refer to the back-of-the-journal resource to discover
how to love those around you well.

Copyright © 2018 Kelly Balarie. All Rights Reserved.

THINGS TO REMEMBER

Copyright © 2018 Kelly Balarie. All Rights Reserved.

HOW THE BOOK *BATTLE READY* IS INSPIRING ME...

MY 3 BIG ETERNITY GOALS...

God, what are you calling me to do with my life?

one

two

three

WHAT TO DO TODAY...

God, what little steps should I take today to see these things through?

one

IDEA:

HOW I'LL DO IT:

WHEN/HOW I'LL KNOW THIS IS COMPLETE:

two

IDEA:

HOW I'LL DO IT:

WHEN/HOW I'LL KNOW THIS IS COMPLETE:

three

IDEA:

HOW I'LL DO IT:

WHEN/HOW I'LL KNOW THIS IS COMPLETE:

You, dear children, are from God and have overcome them, because the one who is in you is greater than the one who is in the world.

1 JOHN 4:4, NIV

GETTING NEGATIVITY & MISTRUTHS OUTTA THE WAY...

God, what negative mental thoughts might arise as I press into these goals?

I won't let them impact my day, because I am preparing my mind to believe...

NOW I PRAY...

...AND TRUST GOD ALONG THE WAY.

What might I experience by following God's plan above, today? What fruit and life might it produce in the future?

HOW THE BOOK *BATTLE READY* IS INSPIRING ME...

MY 3 BIG ETERNITY GOALS...

God, what are you calling me to do with my life?

one

two

three

WHAT TO DO TODAY...

God, what little steps should I take today to see these things through?

one

IDEA:

HOW I'LL DO IT:

WHEN/HOW I'LL KNOW THIS IS COMPLETE:

two

IDEA:

HOW I'LL DO IT:

WHEN/HOW I'LL KNOW THIS IS COMPLETE:

three

IDEA:

HOW I'LL DO IT:

WHEN/HOW I'LL KNOW THIS IS COMPLETE:

GETTING NEGATIVITY & MISTRUTHS OUTTA THE WAY...

God, what negative mental thoughts might arise as I press into these goals?

I won't let them impact my day, because I am preparing my mind to believe...

NOW I PRAY...

...AND TRUST GOD ALONG THE WAY.

What might I experience by following God's plan above, today? What fruit and life might it produce in the future?

HOW THE BOOK *BATTLE READY* IS INSPIRING ME...

MY 3 BIG ETERNITY GOALS...

God, what are you calling me to do with my life?

one

two

three

WHAT TO DO TODAY...

God, what little steps should I take today to see these things through?

one

IDEA:

HOW I'LL DO IT:

WHEN/HOW I'LL KNOW THIS IS COMPLETE:

two

IDEA:

HOW I'LL DO IT:

WHEN/HOW I'LL KNOW THIS IS COMPLETE:

three

IDEA:

HOW I'LL DO IT:

WHEN/HOW I'LL KNOW THIS IS COMPLETE:

*Though an army besiege me, my heart will not fear;
though war break out against me, even then I will be confident.*

PSALM 27:3, NIV

GETTING NEGATIVITY & MISTRUTHS OUTTA THE WAY...

God, what negative mental thoughts might arise as I press into these goals?

I won't let them impact my day, because I am preparing my mind to believe...

NOW I PRAY...

...AND TRUST GOD ALONG THE WAY.

What might I experience by following God's plan above, today? What fruit and life might it produce in the future?

HOW THE BOOK *BATTLE READY* IS INSPIRING ME...

MY 3 BIG ETERNITY GOALS...

God, what are you calling me to do with my life?

one

two

three

WHAT TO DO TODAY...

God, what little steps should I take today to see these things through?

one

IDEA:

HOW I'LL DO IT:

WHEN/HOW I'LL KNOW THIS IS COMPLETE:

two

IDEA:

HOW I'LL DO IT:

WHEN/HOW I'LL KNOW THIS IS COMPLETE:

three

IDEA:

HOW I'LL DO IT:

WHEN/HOW I'LL KNOW THIS IS COMPLETE:

God can make up for wasted-years in a split-second.
KELLY BALARIE, BATTLE READY

GETTING NEGATIVITY & MISTRUTHS OUTTA THE WAY...

God, what negative mental thoughts might arise as I press into these goals?

I won't let them impact my day, because I am preparing my mind to believe...

NOW I PRAY...

...AND TRUST GOD ALONG THE WAY.

What might I experience by following God's plan above, today? What fruit and life might it produce in the future?

HOW THE BOOK *BATTLE READY* IS INSPIRING ME...

MY 3 BIG ETERNITY GOALS...

God, what are you calling me to do with my life?

one

two

three

WHAT TO DO TODAY...

God, what little steps should I take today to see these things through?

one

IDEA:

HOW I'LL DO IT:

WHEN/HOW I'LL KNOW THIS IS COMPLETE:

two

IDEA:

HOW I'LL DO IT:

WHEN/HOW I'LL KNOW THIS IS COMPLETE:

three

IDEA:

HOW I'LL DO IT:

WHEN/HOW I'LL KNOW THIS IS COMPLETE:

> *Be alert and of sober mind. Your enemy the devil prowls around like a roaring lion looking for someone to devour. Resist him, standing firm in the faith, because you know that the family of believers throughout the world is undergoing the same kind of sufferings.*
>
> **1 PETER 5:8-9, NIV**

GETTING NEGATIVITY & MISTRUTHS OUTTA THE WAY...

God, what negative mental thoughts might arise as I press into these goals?

I won't let them impact my day, because I am preparing my mind to believe...

NOW I PRAY...

...AND TRUST GOD ALONG THE WAY.

What might I experience by following God's plan above, today? What fruit and life might it produce in the future?

HOW THE BOOK *BATTLE READY* IS INSPIRING ME...

MY 3 BIG ETERNITY GOALS...

God, what are you calling me to do with my life?

one

two

three

WHAT TO DO TODAY...

God, what little steps should I take today to see these things through?

one

IDEA:

HOW I'LL DO IT:

WHEN/HOW I'LL KNOW THIS IS COMPLETE:

two

IDEA:

HOW I'LL DO IT:

WHEN/HOW I'LL KNOW THIS IS COMPLETE:

three

IDEA:

HOW I'LL DO IT:

WHEN/HOW I'LL KNOW THIS IS COMPLETE:

Women who are prepared with the right thoughts, don't become ruled by the bad.
KELLY BALARIE, BATTLE READY

GETTING NEGATIVITY & MISTRUTHS OUTTA THE WAY...

God, what negative mental thoughts might arise as I press into these goals?

I won't let them impact my day, because I am preparing my mind to believe...

NOW I PRAY...

...AND TRUST GOD ALONG THE WAY.

What might I experience by following God's plan above, today? What fruit and life might it produce in the future?

HOW THE BOOK *BATTLE READY* IS INSPIRING ME...

MY 3 BIG ETERNITY GOALS...

God, what are you calling me to do with my life?

one

two

three

WHAT TO DO TODAY...

God, what little steps should I take today to see these things through?

one

IDEA:

HOW I'LL DO IT:

WHEN/HOW I'LL KNOW THIS IS COMPLETE:

two

IDEA:

HOW I'LL DO IT:

WHEN/HOW I'LL KNOW THIS IS COMPLETE:

three

IDEA:

HOW I'LL DO IT:

WHEN/HOW I'LL KNOW THIS IS COMPLETE:

GETTING NEGATIVITY & MISTRUTHS OUTTA THE WAY...

God, what negative mental thoughts might arise as I press into these goals?

I won't let them impact my day, because I am preparing my mind to believe...

NOW I PRAY...

...AND TRUST GOD ALONG THE WAY.

What might I experience by following God's plan above, today? What fruit and life might it produce in the future?

HOW THE BOOK *BATTLE READY* IS INSPIRING ME...

MY 3 BIG ETERNITY GOALS...

God, what are you calling me to do with my life?

one

two

three

WHAT TO DO TODAY...

God, what little steps should I take today to see these things through?

one

IDEA:

HOW I'LL DO IT:

WHEN/HOW I'LL KNOW THIS IS COMPLETE:

two

IDEA:

HOW I'LL DO IT:

WHEN/HOW I'LL KNOW THIS IS COMPLETE:

three

IDEA:

HOW I'LL DO IT:

WHEN/HOW I'LL KNOW THIS IS COMPLETE:

If humility never tries, it is always in error.
KELLY BALARIE, BATTLE READY

GETTING NEGATIVITY & MISTRUTHS OUTTA THE WAY...

God, what negative mental thoughts might arise as I press into these goals?

I won't let them impact my day, because I am preparing my mind to believe...

NOW I PRAY...

...AND TRUST GOD ALONG THE WAY.

What might I experience by following God's plan above, today? What fruit and life might it produce in the future?

HOW THE BOOK *BATTLE READY* IS INSPIRING ME...

MY 3 BIG ETERNITY GOALS...

God, what are you calling me to do with my life?

one

two

three

WHAT TO DO TODAY...

God, what little steps should I take today to see these things through?

one

IDEA:

HOW I'LL DO IT:

WHEN/HOW I'LL KNOW THIS IS COMPLETE:

two

IDEA:

HOW I'LL DO IT:

WHEN/HOW I'LL KNOW THIS IS COMPLETE:

three

IDEA:

HOW I'LL DO IT:

WHEN/HOW I'LL KNOW THIS IS COMPLETE:

Blessed is the one who perseveres under trial because, having stood the test, that person will receive the crown of life that the Lord has promised to those who love him.

JAMES 1:12, NIV

GETTING NEGATIVITY & MISTRUTHS OUTTA THE WAY...

God, what negative mental thoughts might arise as I press into these goals?

I won't let them impact my day, because I am preparing my mind to believe...

NOW I PRAY...

...AND TRUST GOD ALONG THE WAY.

What might I experience by following God's plan above, today? What fruit and life might it produce in the future?

HOW THE BOOK *BATTLE READY* IS INSPIRING ME...

MY 3 BIG ETERNITY GOALS...

God, what are you calling me to do with my life?

one

two

three

WHAT TO DO TODAY...

God, what little steps should I take today to see these things through?

one

IDEA:

HOW I'LL DO IT:

WHEN/HOW I'LL KNOW THIS IS COMPLETE:

two

IDEA:

HOW I'LL DO IT:

WHEN/HOW I'LL KNOW THIS IS COMPLETE:

three

IDEA:

HOW I'LL DO IT:

WHEN/HOW I'LL KNOW THIS IS COMPLETE:

Say, "God, I am all in. I'll do anything for you.
You are the matter that most matters."
KELLY BALARIE, BATTLE READY

GETTING NEGATIVITY & MISTRUTHS OUTTA THE WAY...

God, what negative mental thoughts might arise as I press into these goals?

I won't let them impact my day, because I am preparing my mind to believe...

NOW I PRAY...

...AND TRUST GOD ALONG THE WAY.

What might I experience by following God's plan above, today? What fruit and life might it produce in the future?

HOW THE BOOK *BATTLE READY* IS INSPIRING ME...

MY 3 BIG ETERNITY GOALS...

God, what are you calling me to do with my life?

one

two

three

WHAT TO DO TODAY...

God, what little steps should I take today to see these things through?

one

IDEA:

HOW I'LL DO IT:

WHEN/HOW I'LL KNOW THIS IS COMPLETE:

two

IDEA:

HOW I'LL DO IT:

WHEN/HOW I'LL KNOW THIS IS COMPLETE:

three

IDEA:

HOW I'LL DO IT:

WHEN/HOW I'LL KNOW THIS IS COMPLETE:

> *They triumphed over him by the blood of the Lamb and by the word of their testimony; they did not love their lives so much as to shrink from death.*
>
> **REVELATION 12:11, NIV**

GETTING NEGATIVITY & MISTRUTHS OUTTA THE WAY...

God, what negative mental thoughts might arise as I press into these goals?

I won't let them impact my day, because I am preparing my mind to believe...

NOW I PRAY...

...AND TRUST GOD ALONG THE WAY.

What might I experience by following God's plan above, today? What fruit and life might it produce in the future?

HOW THE BOOK *BATTLE READY* IS INSPIRING ME...

MY 3 BIG ETERNITY GOALS...

God, what are you calling me to do with my life?

one

two

three

WHAT TO DO TODAY...

God, what little steps should I take today to see these things through?

one

IDEA:

HOW I'LL DO IT:

WHEN/HOW I'LL KNOW THIS IS COMPLETE:

two

IDEA:

HOW I'LL DO IT:

WHEN/HOW I'LL KNOW THIS IS COMPLETE:

three

IDEA:

HOW I'LL DO IT:

WHEN/HOW I'LL KNOW THIS IS COMPLETE:

GETTING NEGATIVITY & MISTRUTHS OUTTA THE WAY...

God, what negative mental thoughts might arise as I press into these goals?

I won't let them impact my day, because I am preparing my mind to believe...

NOW I PRAY...

...AND TRUST GOD ALONG THE WAY.

What might I experience by following God's plan above, today? What fruit and life might it produce in the future?

HOW THE BOOK *BATTLE READY* IS INSPIRING ME...

MY 3 BIG ETERNITY GOALS...

God, what are you calling me to do with my life?

one

Two

Three

WHAT TO DO TODAY...

God, what little steps should I take today to see these things through?

one

IDEA:

HOW I'LL DO IT:

WHEN/HOW I'LL KNOW THIS IS COMPLETE:

Two

IDEA:

HOW I'LL DO IT:

WHEN/HOW I'LL KNOW THIS IS COMPLETE:

Three

IDEA:

HOW I'LL DO IT:

WHEN/HOW I'LL KNOW THIS IS COMPLETE:

We demolish arguments and every pretension that sets itself up against the knowledge of God, and we take captive every thought to make it obedient to Christ.

2 CORINTHIANS 10:5, NIV

GETTING NEGATIVITY & MISTRUTHS OUTTA THE WAY...

God, what negative mental thoughts might arise as I press into these goals?

I won't let them impact my day, because I am preparing my mind to believe...

NOW I PRAY...

...AND TRUST GOD ALONG THE WAY.

What might I experience by following God's plan above, today? What fruit and life might it produce in the future?

HOW THE BOOK *BATTLE READY* IS INSPIRING ME...

MY 3 BIG ETERNITY GOALS...

God, what are you calling me to do with my life?

one

two

three

WHAT TO DO TODAY...

God, what little steps should I take today to see these things through?

one

IDEA:

HOW I'LL DO IT:

WHEN/HOW I'LL KNOW THIS IS COMPLETE:

two

IDEA:

HOW I'LL DO IT:

WHEN/HOW I'LL KNOW THIS IS COMPLETE:

three

IDEA:

HOW I'LL DO IT:

WHEN/HOW I'LL KNOW THIS IS COMPLETE:

GETTING NEGATIVITY & MISTRUTHS OUTTA THE WAY...

God, what negative mental thoughts might arise as I press into these goals?

I won't let them impact my day, because I am preparing my mind to believe...

NOW I PRAY...

...AND TRUST GOD ALONG THE WAY.

What might I experience by following God's plan above, today? What fruit and life might it produce in the future?

HOW THE BOOK *BATTLE READY* IS INSPIRING ME...

MY 3 BIG ETERNITY GOALS...

God, what are you calling me to do with my life?

one

two

three

WHAT TO DO TODAY...

God, what little steps should I take today to see these things through?

one

IDEA:

HOW I'LL DO IT:

WHEN/HOW I'LL KNOW THIS IS COMPLETE:

two

IDEA:

HOW I'LL DO IT:

WHEN/HOW I'LL KNOW THIS IS COMPLETE:

three

IDEA:

HOW I'LL DO IT:

WHEN/HOW I'LL KNOW THIS IS COMPLETE:

GETTING NEGATIVITY & MISTRUTHS OUTTA THE WAY...

God, what negative mental thoughts might arise as I press into these goals?

I won't let them impact my day, because I am preparing my mind to believe...

NOW I PRAY...

...AND TRUST GOD ALONG THE WAY.

What might I experience by following God's plan above, today? What fruit and life might it produce in the future?

HOW THE BOOK *BATTLE READY* IS INSPIRING ME...

MY 3 BIG ETERNITY GOALS...

God, what are you calling me to do with my life?

one

two

three

WHAT TO DO TODAY...

God, what little steps should I take today to see these things through?

one

IDEA:

HOW I'LL DO IT:

WHEN/HOW I'LL KNOW THIS IS COMPLETE:

two

IDEA:

HOW I'LL DO IT:

WHEN/HOW I'LL KNOW THIS IS COMPLETE:

three

IDEA:

HOW I'LL DO IT:

WHEN/HOW I'LL KNOW THIS IS COMPLETE:

GETTING NEGATIVITY & MISTRUTHS OUTTA THE WAY...

God, what negative mental thoughts might arise as I press into these goals?

I won't let them impact my day, because I am preparing my mind to believe...

NOW I PRAY...

...AND TRUST GOD ALONG THE WAY.

What might I experience by following God's plan above, today? What fruit and life might it produce in the future?

HOW THE BOOK *BATTLE READY* IS INSPIRING ME...

MY 3 BIG ETERNITY GOALS...

God, what are you calling me to do with my life?

one

two

three

WHAT TO DO TODAY...

God, what little steps should I take today to see these things through?

one

IDEA:

HOW I'LL DO IT:

WHEN/HOW I'LL KNOW THIS IS COMPLETE:

two

IDEA:

HOW I'LL DO IT:

WHEN/HOW I'LL KNOW THIS IS COMPLETE:

three

IDEA:

HOW I'LL DO IT:

WHEN/HOW I'LL KNOW THIS IS COMPLETE:

> *Fight the good fight of the faith. Take hold of the eternal life to which you were called when you made your good confession in the presence of many witnesses.*
> 1 TIMOTHY 6:12, NIV

GETTING NEGATIVITY & MISTRUTHS OUTTA THE WAY...

God, what negative mental thoughts might arise as I press into these goals?

I won't let them impact my day, because I am preparing my mind to believe...

NOW I PRAY...

...AND TRUST GOD ALONG THE WAY.

What might I experience by following God's plan above, today? What fruit and life might it produce in the future?

HOW THE BOOK *BATTLE READY* IS INSPIRING ME...

MY 3 BIG ETERNITY GOALS...

God, what are you calling me to do with my life?

one

two

three

WHAT TO DO TODAY...

God, what little steps should I take today to see these things through?

one

IDEA:

HOW I'LL DO IT:

WHEN/HOW I'LL KNOW THIS IS COMPLETE:

two

IDEA:

HOW I'LL DO IT:

WHEN/HOW I'LL KNOW THIS IS COMPLETE:

three

IDEA:

HOW I'LL DO IT:

WHEN/HOW I'LL KNOW THIS IS COMPLETE:

GETTING NEGATIVITY & MISTRUTHS OUTTA THE WAY...

God, what negative mental thoughts might arise as I press into these goals?

I won't let them impact my day, because I am preparing my mind to believe...

NOW I PRAY...

...AND TRUST GOD ALONG THE WAY.

What might I experience by following God's plan above, today? What fruit and life might it produce in the future?

HOW THE BOOK *BATTLE READY* IS INSPIRING ME...

MY 3 BIG ETERNITY GOALS...

God, what are you calling me to do with my life?

one

two

three

WHAT TO DO TODAY...

God, what little steps should I take today to see these things through?

one

IDEA:

HOW I'LL DO IT:

WHEN/HOW I'LL KNOW THIS IS COMPLETE:

Two

IDEA:

HOW I'LL DO IT:

WHEN/HOW I'LL KNOW THIS IS COMPLETE:

three

IDEA:

HOW I'LL DO IT:

WHEN/HOW I'LL KNOW THIS IS COMPLETE:

The LORD is my light and my salvation-- whom shall I fear?
The LORD is the stronghold of my life-- of whom shall I be afraid?
PSALM 27:1, NIV

GETTING NEGATIVITY & MISTRUTHS OUTTA THE WAY...

God, what negative mental thoughts might arise as I press into these goals?

I won't let them impact my day, because I am preparing my mind to believe...

NOW I PRAY...

...AND TRUST GOD ALONG THE WAY.

What might I experience by following God's plan above, today? What fruit and life might it produce in the future?

HOW THE BOOK *BATTLE READY* IS INSPIRING ME...

MY 3 BIG ETERNITY GOALS...

God, what are you calling me to do with my life?

one

two

three

WHAT TO DO TODAY...

God, what little steps should I take today to see these things through?

one

IDEA:

HOW I'LL DO IT:

WHEN/HOW I'LL KNOW THIS IS COMPLETE:

two

IDEA:

HOW I'LL DO IT:

WHEN/HOW I'LL KNOW THIS IS COMPLETE:

three

IDEA:

HOW I'LL DO IT:

WHEN/HOW I'LL KNOW THIS IS COMPLETE:

GETTING NEGATIVITY & MISTRUTHS OUTTA THE WAY...

God, what negative mental thoughts might arise as I press into these goals?

I won't let them impact my day, because I am preparing my mind to believe...

NOW I PRAY...

...AND TRUST GOD ALONG THE WAY.

What might I experience by following God's plan above, today? What fruit and life might it produce in the future?

HOW THE BOOK *BATTLE READY* IS INSPIRING ME...

MY 3 BIG ETERNITY GOALS...

God, what are you calling me to do with my life?

one

two

three

WHAT TO DO TODAY...

God, what little steps should I take today to see these things through?

one

IDEA:

HOW I'LL DO IT:

WHEN/HOW I'LL KNOW THIS IS COMPLETE:

two

IDEA:

HOW I'LL DO IT:

WHEN/HOW I'LL KNOW THIS IS COMPLETE:

three

IDEA:

HOW I'LL DO IT:

WHEN/HOW I'LL KNOW THIS IS COMPLETE:

GETTING NEGATIVITY & MISTRUTHS OUTTA THE WAY...

God, what negative mental thoughts might arise as I press into these goals?

I won't let them impact my day, because I am preparing my mind to believe...

NOW I PRAY...

...AND TRUST GOD ALONG THE WAY.

What might I experience by following God's plan above, today? What fruit and life might it produce in the future?

HOW THE BOOK *BATTLE READY* IS INSPIRING ME...

MY 3 BIG ETERNITY GOALS...

God, what are you calling me to do with my life?

one

two

three

WHAT TO DO TODAY...

God, what little steps should I take today to see these things through?

one

IDEA:

HOW I'LL DO IT:

WHEN/HOW I'LL KNOW THIS IS COMPLETE:

two

IDEA:

HOW I'LL DO IT:

WHEN/HOW I'LL KNOW THIS IS COMPLETE:

three

IDEA:

HOW I'LL DO IT:

WHEN/HOW I'LL KNOW THIS IS COMPLETE:

GETTING NEGATIVITY & MISTRUTHS OUTTA THE WAY...

God, what negative mental thoughts might arise as I press into these goals?

I won't let them impact my day, because I am preparing my mind to believe...

NOW I PRAY...

...AND TRUST GOD ALONG THE WAY.

What might I experience by following God's plan above, today? What fruit and life might it produce in the future?

HOW THE BOOK *BATTLE READY* IS INSPIRING ME...

MY 3 BIG ETERNITY GOALS...

God, what are you calling me to do with my life?

one

two

three

WHAT TO DO TODAY...

God, what little steps should I take today to see these things through?

one

IDEA:

HOW I'LL DO IT:

WHEN/HOW I'LL KNOW THIS IS COMPLETE:

two

IDEA:

HOW I'LL DO IT:

WHEN/HOW I'LL KNOW THIS IS COMPLETE:

three

IDEA:

HOW I'LL DO IT:

WHEN/HOW I'LL KNOW THIS IS COMPLETE:

GETTING NEGATIVITY & MISTRUTHS OUTTA THE WAY...

God, what negative mental thoughts might arise as I press into these goals?

I won't let them impact my day, because I am preparing my mind to believe...

NOW I PRAY...

...AND TRUST GOD ALONG THE WAY.

What might I experience by following God's plan above, today? What fruit and life might it produce in the future?

HOW THE BOOK *BATTLE READY* IS INSPIRING ME...

MY 3 BIG ETERNITY GOALS...

God, what are you calling me to do with my life?

one

two

three

WHAT TO DO TODAY...

God, what little steps should I take today to see these things through?

one

IDEA:

HOW I'LL DO IT:

WHEN/HOW I'LL KNOW THIS IS COMPLETE:

two

IDEA:

HOW I'LL DO IT:

WHEN/HOW I'LL KNOW THIS IS COMPLETE:

three

IDEA:

HOW I'LL DO IT:

WHEN/HOW I'LL KNOW THIS IS COMPLETE:

Huge endings happen because of small beginnings.
KELLY BALARIE, BATTLE READY

GETTING NEGATIVITY & MISTRUTHS OUTTA THE WAY...

God, what negative mental thoughts might arise as I press into these goals?

I won't let them impact my day, because I am preparing my mind to believe...

NOW I PRAY...

...AND TRUST GOD ALONG THE WAY.

What might I experience by following God's plan above, today? What fruit and life might it produce in the future?

HOW THE BOOK *BATTLE READY* IS INSPIRING ME...

MY 3 BIG ETERNITY GOALS...

God, what are you calling me to do with my life?

one

two

three

WHAT TO DO TODAY...

God, what little steps should I take today to see these things through?

one

IDEA:

HOW I'LL DO IT:

WHEN/HOW I'LL KNOW THIS IS COMPLETE:

two

IDEA:

HOW I'LL DO IT:

WHEN/HOW I'LL KNOW THIS IS COMPLETE:

three

IDEA:

HOW I'LL DO IT:

WHEN/HOW I'LL KNOW THIS IS COMPLETE:

GETTING NEGATIVITY & MISTRUTHS OUTTA THE WAY...

God, what negative mental thoughts might arise as I press into these goals?

I won't let them impact my day, because I am preparing my mind to believe...

NOW I PRAY...

...AND TRUST GOD ALONG THE WAY.

What might I experience by following God's plan above, today? What fruit and life might it produce in the future?

HOW THE BOOK *BATTLE READY* IS INSPIRING ME...

MY 3 BIG ETERNITY GOALS...

God, what are you calling me to do with my life?

one

two

three

WHAT TO DO TODAY...

God, what little steps should I take today to see these things through?

one

IDEA:

HOW I'LL DO IT:

WHEN/HOW I'LL KNOW THIS IS COMPLETE:

two

IDEA:

HOW I'LL DO IT:

WHEN/HOW I'LL KNOW THIS IS COMPLETE:

three

IDEA:

HOW I'LL DO IT:

WHEN/HOW I'LL KNOW THIS IS COMPLETE:

GETTING NEGATIVITY & MISTRUTHS OUTTA THE WAY...

God, what negative mental thoughts might arise as I press into these goals?

I won't let them impact my day, because I am preparing my mind to believe...

NOW I PRAY...

...AND TRUST GOD ALONG THE WAY.

What might I experience by following God's plan above, today? What fruit and life might it produce in the future?

HOW THE BOOK *BATTLE READY* IS INSPIRING ME...

MY 3 BIG ETERNITY GOALS...

God, what are you calling me to do with my life?

one

two

three

WHAT TO DO TODAY...

God, what little steps should I take today to see these things through?

one

IDEA:

HOW I'LL DO IT:

WHEN/HOW I'LL KNOW THIS IS COMPLETE:

two

IDEA:

HOW I'LL DO IT:

WHEN/HOW I'LL KNOW THIS IS COMPLETE:

three

IDEA:

HOW I'LL DO IT:

WHEN/HOW I'LL KNOW THIS IS COMPLETE:

There is no fear in love; but perfect love casts out fear, because fear involves punishment, and the one who fears is not perfected in love.

1 JOHN 4:18, NIV

GETTING NEGATIVITY & MISTRUTHS OUTTA THE WAY...

God, what negative mental thoughts might arise as I press into these goals?

I won't let them impact my day, because I am preparing my mind to believe...

NOW I PRAY...

...AND TRUST GOD ALONG THE WAY.

What might I experience by following God's plan above, today? What fruit and life might it produce in the future?

HOW THE BOOK *BATTLE READY* IS INSPIRING ME...

MY 3 BIG ETERNITY GOALS...

God, what are you calling me to do with my life?

one

two

three

WHAT TO DO TODAY...

God, what little steps should I take today to see these things through?

one

IDEA:

HOW I'LL DO IT:

WHEN/HOW I'LL KNOW THIS IS COMPLETE:

two

IDEA:

HOW I'LL DO IT:

WHEN/HOW I'LL KNOW THIS IS COMPLETE:

three

IDEA:

HOW I'LL DO IT:

WHEN/HOW I'LL KNOW THIS IS COMPLETE:

GETTING NEGATIVITY & MISTRUTHS OUTTA THE WAY...

God, what negative mental thoughts might arise as I press into these goals?

I won't let them impact my day, because I am preparing my mind to believe...

NOW I PRAY...

...AND TRUST GOD ALONG THE WAY.

What might I experience by following God's plan above, today? What fruit and life might it produce in the future?

HOW THE BOOK *BATTLE READY* IS INSPIRING ME...

MY 3 BIG ETERNITY GOALS...

God, what are you calling me to do with my life?

one

two

three

WHAT TO DO TODAY...

God, what little steps should I take today to see these things through?

one

IDEA:

HOW I'LL DO IT:

WHEN/HOW I'LL KNOW THIS IS COMPLETE:

two

IDEA:

HOW I'LL DO IT:

WHEN/HOW I'LL KNOW THIS IS COMPLETE:

three

IDEA:

HOW I'LL DO IT:

WHEN/HOW I'LL KNOW THIS IS COMPLETE:

I will go before you and will level the mountains; I will break down gates of bronze and cut through bars of iron.

ISAIAH 45:2, NIV

GETTING NEGATIVITY & MISTRUTHS OUTTA THE WAY...

God, what negative mental thoughts might arise as I press into these goals?

I won't let them impact my day, because I am preparing my mind to believe...

NOW I PRAY...

...AND TRUST GOD ALONG THE WAY.

What might I experience by following God's plan above, today? What fruit and life might it produce in the future?

HOW THE BOOK *BATTLE READY* IS INSPIRING ME...

MY 3 BIG ETERNITY GOALS...

God, what are you calling me to do with my life?

one

two

three

WHAT TO DO TODAY...

God, what little steps should I take today to see these things through?

one

IDEA:

HOW I'LL DO IT:

WHEN/HOW I'LL KNOW THIS IS COMPLETE:

two

IDEA:

HOW I'LL DO IT:

WHEN/HOW I'LL KNOW THIS IS COMPLETE:

three

IDEA:

HOW I'LL DO IT:

WHEN/HOW I'LL KNOW THIS IS COMPLETE:

GETTING NEGATIVITY & MISTRUTHS OUTTA THE WAY...

God, what negative mental thoughts might arise as I press into these goals?

I won't let them impact my day, because I am preparing my mind to believe...

NOW I PRAY...

...AND TRUST GOD ALONG THE WAY.

What might I experience by following God's plan above, today? What fruit and life might it produce in the future?

HOW THE BOOK *BATTLE READY* IS INSPIRING ME...

MY 3 BIG ETERNITY GOALS...

God, what are you calling me to do with my life?

one

two

three

WHAT TO DO TODAY...

God, what little steps should I take today to see these things through?

one

IDEA:

HOW I'LL DO IT:

WHEN/HOW I'LL KNOW THIS IS COMPLETE:

two

IDEA:

HOW I'LL DO IT:

WHEN/HOW I'LL KNOW THIS IS COMPLETE:

three

IDEA:

HOW I'LL DO IT:

WHEN/HOW I'LL KNOW THIS IS COMPLETE:

Have I not commanded you? Be strong and courageous! Do not tremble or be dismayed, for the Lord your God is with you wherever you go.
JOSHUA 1:9, NIV

GETTING NEGATIVITY & MISTRUTHS OUTTA THE WAY...

God, what negative mental thoughts might arise as I press into these goals?

I won't let them impact my day, because I am preparing my mind to believe...

NOW I PRAY...

...AND TRUST GOD ALONG THE WAY.

What might I experience by following God's plan above, today? What fruit and life might it produce in the future?

HOW THE BOOK *BATTLE READY* IS INSPIRING ME...

MY 3 BIG ETERNITY GOALS...

God, what are you calling me to do with my life?

one

two

three

WHAT TO DO TODAY...

God, what little steps should I take today to see these things through?

one

IDEA:

HOW I'LL DO IT:

WHEN/HOW I'LL KNOW THIS IS COMPLETE:

Two

IDEA:

HOW I'LL DO IT:

WHEN/HOW I'LL KNOW THIS IS COMPLETE:

three

IDEA:

HOW I'LL DO IT:

WHEN/HOW I'LL KNOW THIS IS COMPLETE:

GETTING NEGATIVITY & MISTRUTHS OUTTA THE WAY...

God, what negative mental thoughts might arise as I press into these goals?

I won't let them impact my day, because I am preparing my mind to believe...

NOW I PRAY...

...AND TRUST GOD ALONG THE WAY.

What might I experience by following God's plan above, today? What fruit and life might it produce in the future?

HOW THE BOOK *BATTLE READY* IS INSPIRING ME...

MY 3 BIG ETERNITY GOALS...

God, what are you calling me to do with my life?

one

two

three

WHAT TO DO TODAY...

God, what little steps should I take today to see these things through?

one

IDEA:

HOW I'LL DO IT:

WHEN/HOW I'LL KNOW THIS IS COMPLETE:

two

IDEA:

HOW I'LL DO IT:

WHEN/HOW I'LL KNOW THIS IS COMPLETE:

three

IDEA:

HOW I'LL DO IT:

WHEN/HOW I'LL KNOW THIS IS COMPLETE:

"Not by might nor by power, but by my Spirit," says the LORD Almighty.
ZECHARIAH 4:6, NIV

GETTING NEGATIVITY & MISTRUTHS OUTTA THE WAY...

God, what negative mental thoughts might arise as I press into these goals?

I won't let them impact my day, because I am preparing my mind to believe...

NOW I PRAY...

...AND TRUST GOD ALONG THE WAY.

What might I experience by following God's plan above, today? What fruit and life might it produce in the future?

HOW THE BOOK *BATTLE READY* IS INSPIRING ME...

MY 3 BIG ETERNITY GOALS...

God, what are you calling me to do with my life?

one

two

three

WHAT TO DO TODAY...

God, what little steps should I take today to see these things through?

one

IDEA:

HOW I'LL DO IT:

WHEN/HOW I'LL KNOW THIS IS COMPLETE:

two

IDEA:

HOW I'LL DO IT:

WHEN/HOW I'LL KNOW THIS IS COMPLETE:

three

IDEA:

HOW I'LL DO IT:

WHEN/HOW I'LL KNOW THIS IS COMPLETE:

What if you actually started to believe God has good gifts for you because you are His beloved daughter?
KELLY BALARIE, BATTLE READY

GETTING NEGATIVITY & MISTRUTHS OUTTA THE WAY...

God, what negative mental thoughts might arise as I press into these goals?

I won't let them impact my day, because I am preparing my mind to believe...

NOW I PRAY...

...AND TRUST GOD ALONG THE WAY.

What might I experience by following God's plan above, today? What fruit and life might it produce in the future?

HOW THE BOOK *BATTLE READY* IS INSPIRING ME...

MY 3 BIG ETERNITY GOALS...

God, what are you calling me to do with my life?

one

two

three

WHAT TO DO TODAY...

God, what little steps should I take today to see these things through?

one

IDEA:

HOW I'LL DO IT:

WHEN/HOW I'LL KNOW THIS IS COMPLETE:

two

IDEA:

HOW I'LL DO IT:

WHEN/HOW I'LL KNOW THIS IS COMPLETE:

three

IDEA:

HOW I'LL DO IT:

WHEN/HOW I'LL KNOW THIS IS COMPLETE:

*I have given you authority to trample on snakes and scorpions
and to overcome all the power of the enemy; nothing will harm you.*

LUKE 10:19, NIV

GETTING NEGATIVITY & MISTRUTHS OUTTA THE WAY...

God, what negative mental thoughts might arise as I press into these goals?

I won't let them impact my day, because I am preparing my mind to believe...

NOW I PRAY...

...AND TRUST GOD ALONG THE WAY.

*What might I experience by following God's plan above, today? What fruit and life might
it produce in the future?*

HOW THE BOOK *BATTLE READY* IS INSPIRING ME...

MY 3 BIG ETERNITY GOALS...

God, what are you calling me to do with my life?

one

two

three

WHAT TO DO TODAY...

God, what little steps should I take today to see these things through?

one

IDEA:

HOW I'LL DO IT:

WHEN/HOW I'LL KNOW THIS IS COMPLETE:

two

IDEA:

HOW I'LL DO IT:

WHEN/HOW I'LL KNOW THIS IS COMPLETE:

three

IDEA:

HOW I'LL DO IT:

WHEN/HOW I'LL KNOW THIS IS COMPLETE:

*The most powerful woman in the world is
the one operating right where God wants her.*
KELLY BALARIE, BATTLE READY

GETTING NEGATIVITY & MISTRUTHS OUTTA THE WAY...

God, what negative mental thoughts might arise as I press into these goals?

I won't let them impact my day, because I am preparing my mind to believe...

NOW I PRAY...

...AND TRUST GOD ALONG THE WAY.

*What might I experience by following God's plan above, today? What fruit and life might
it produce in the future?*

HOW THE BOOK *BATTLE READY* IS INSPIRING ME...

MY 3 BIG ETERNITY GOALS...

God, what are you calling me to do with my life?

one

two

three

WHAT TO DO TODAY...

God, what little steps should I take today to see these things through?

one

IDEA:

HOW I'LL DO IT:

WHEN/HOW I'LL KNOW THIS IS COMPLETE:

two

IDEA:

HOW I'LL DO IT:

WHEN/HOW I'LL KNOW THIS IS COMPLETE:

three

IDEA:

HOW I'LL DO IT:

WHEN/HOW I'LL KNOW THIS IS COMPLETE:

GETTING NEGATIVITY & MISTRUTHS OUTTA THE WAY...

God, what negative mental thoughts might arise as I press into these goals?

I won't let them impact my day, because I am preparing my mind to believe...

NOW I PRAY...

...AND TRUST GOD ALONG THE WAY.

What might I experience by following God's plan above, today? What fruit and life might it produce in the future?

HOW THE BOOK *BATTLE READY* IS INSPIRING ME...

MY 3 BIG ETERNITY GOALS...

God, what are you calling me to do with my life?

one

two

three

WHAT TO DO TODAY...

God, what little steps should I take today to see these things through?

one

IDEA:

HOW I'LL DO IT:

WHEN/HOW I'LL KNOW THIS IS COMPLETE:

two

IDEA:

HOW I'LL DO IT:

WHEN/HOW I'LL KNOW THIS IS COMPLETE:

three

IDEA:

HOW I'LL DO IT:

WHEN/HOW I'LL KNOW THIS IS COMPLETE:

GETTING NEGATIVITY & MISTRUTHS OUTTA THE WAY...

God, what negative mental thoughts might arise as I press into these goals?

I won't let them impact my day, because I am preparing my mind to believe...

NOW I PRAY...

...AND TRUST GOD ALONG THE WAY.

What might I experience by following God's plan above, today? What fruit and life might it produce in the future?

HOW THE BOOK *BATTLE READY* IS INSPIRING ME...

MY 3 BIG ETERNITY GOALS...

God, what are you calling me to do with my life?

one

two

three

WHAT TO DO TODAY...

God, what little steps should I take today to see these things through?

one

IDEA:

HOW I'LL DO IT:

WHEN/HOW I'LL KNOW THIS IS COMPLETE:

Two

IDEA:

HOW I'LL DO IT:

WHEN/HOW I'LL KNOW THIS IS COMPLETE:

three

IDEA:

HOW I'LL DO IT:

WHEN/HOW I'LL KNOW THIS IS COMPLETE:

GETTING NEGATIVITY & MISTRUTHS OUTTA THE WAY...

God, what negative mental thoughts might arise as I press into these goals?

I won't let them impact my day, because I am preparing my mind to believe...

NOW I PRAY...

...AND TRUST GOD ALONG THE WAY.

What might I experience by following God's plan above, today? What fruit and life might it produce in the future?

HOW THE BOOK *BATTLE READY* IS INSPIRING ME...

MY 3 BIG ETERNITY GOALS...

God, what are you calling me to do with my life?

one

two

three

WHAT TO DO TODAY...

God, what little steps should I take today to see these things through?

one

IDEA:

HOW I'LL DO IT:

WHEN/HOW I'LL KNOW THIS IS COMPLETE:

two

IDEA:

HOW I'LL DO IT:

WHEN/HOW I'LL KNOW THIS IS COMPLETE:

three

IDEA:

HOW I'LL DO IT:

WHEN/HOW I'LL KNOW THIS IS COMPLETE:

GETTING NEGATIVITY & MISTRUTHS OUTTA THE WAY...

God, what negative mental thoughts might arise as I press into these goals?

I won't let them impact my day, because I am preparing my mind to believe...

NOW I PRAY...

...AND TRUST GOD ALONG THE WAY.

What might I experience by following God's plan above, today? What fruit and life might it produce in the future?

HOW THE BOOK *BATTLE READY* IS INSPIRING ME...

MY 3 BIG ETERNITY GOALS...

God, what are you calling me to do with my life?

one

two

three

WHAT TO DO TODAY...

God, what little steps should I take today to see these things through?

one

IDEA:

HOW I'LL DO IT:

WHEN/HOW I'LL KNOW THIS IS COMPLETE:

two

IDEA:

HOW I'LL DO IT:

WHEN/HOW I'LL KNOW THIS IS COMPLETE:

three

IDEA:

HOW I'LL DO IT:

WHEN/HOW I'LL KNOW THIS IS COMPLETE:

This is what the LORD says to you: 'Do not be afraid or discouraged because of this vast army. For the battle is not yours, but God's.
2 CHRONICLES 20:15, NIV

GETTING NEGATIVITY & MISTRUTHS OUTTA THE WAY...

God, what negative mental thoughts might arise as I press into these goals?

I won't let them impact my day, because I am preparing my mind to believe...

NOW I PRAY...

...AND TRUST GOD ALONG THE WAY.

What might I experience by following God's plan above, today? What fruit and life might it produce in the future?

HOW THE BOOK *BATTLE READY* IS INSPIRING ME...

MY 3 BIG ETERNITY GOALS...

God, what are you calling me to do with my life?

one

two

three

WHAT TO DO TODAY...

God, what little steps should I take today to see these things through?

one

IDEA:

HOW I'LL DO IT:

WHEN/HOW I'LL KNOW THIS IS COMPLETE:

Two

IDEA:

HOW I'LL DO IT:

WHEN/HOW I'LL KNOW THIS IS COMPLETE:

three

IDEA:

HOW I'LL DO IT:

WHEN/HOW I'LL KNOW THIS IS COMPLETE:

GETTING NEGATIVITY & MISTRUTHS OUTTA THE WAY...

God, what negative mental thoughts might arise as I press into these goals?

I won't let them impact my day, because I am preparing my mind to believe...

NOW I PRAY...

...AND TRUST GOD ALONG THE WAY.

What might I experience by following God's plan above, today? What fruit and life might it produce in the future?

HOW THE BOOK *BATTLE READY* IS INSPIRING ME...

MY 3 BIG ETERNITY GOALS...

God, what are you calling me to do with my life?

one

two

three

WHAT TO DO TODAY...

God, what little steps should I take today to see these things through?

one

IDEA:

HOW I'LL DO IT:

WHEN/HOW I'LL KNOW THIS IS COMPLETE:

two

IDEA:

HOW I'LL DO IT:

WHEN/HOW I'LL KNOW THIS IS COMPLETE:

three

IDEA:

HOW I'LL DO IT:

WHEN/HOW I'LL KNOW THIS IS COMPLETE:

The LORD will march out like a champion, like a warrior he will stir up his zeal; with a shout he will raise the battle cry and will triumph over his enemies.

ISAIAH 42:13, NIV

GETTING NEGATIVITY & MISTRUTHS OUTTA THE WAY...

God, what negative mental thoughts might arise as I press into these goals?

I won't let them impact my day, because I am preparing my mind to believe...

NOW I PRAY...

...AND TRUST GOD ALONG THE WAY.

What might I experience by following God's plan above, today? What fruit and life might it produce in the future?

HOW THE BOOK *BATTLE READY* IS INSPIRING ME...

MY 3 BIG ETERNITY GOALS...

God, what are you calling me to do with my life?

one

two

three

WHAT TO DO TODAY...

God, what little steps should I take today to see these things through?

one

IDEA:

HOW I'LL DO IT:

WHEN/HOW I'LL KNOW THIS IS COMPLETE:

two

IDEA:

HOW I'LL DO IT:

WHEN/HOW I'LL KNOW THIS IS COMPLETE:

three

IDEA:

HOW I'LL DO IT:

WHEN/HOW I'LL KNOW THIS IS COMPLETE:

GETTING NEGATIVITY & MISTRUTHS OUTTA THE WAY...

God, what negative mental thoughts might arise as I press into these goals?

I won't let them impact my day, because I am preparing my mind to believe...

NOW I PRAY...

...AND TRUST GOD ALONG THE WAY.

What might I experience by following God's plan above, today? What fruit and life might it produce in the future?

HOW THE BOOK *BATTLE READY* IS INSPIRING ME...

MY 3 BIG ETERNITY GOALS...

God, what are you calling me to do with my life?

one

two

three

WHAT TO DO TODAY...

God, what little steps should I take today to see these things through?

one

IDEA:

HOW I'LL DO IT:

WHEN/HOW I'LL KNOW THIS IS COMPLETE:

two

IDEA:

HOW I'LL DO IT:

WHEN/HOW I'LL KNOW THIS IS COMPLETE:

three

IDEA:

HOW I'LL DO IT:

WHEN/HOW I'LL KNOW THIS IS COMPLETE:

GETTING NEGATIVITY & MISTRUTHS OUTTA THE WAY...

God, what negative mental thoughts might arise as I press into these goals?

I won't let them impact my day, because I am preparing my mind to believe...

NOW I PRAY...

...AND TRUST GOD ALONG THE WAY.

What might I experience by following God's plan above, today? What fruit and life might it produce in the future?

HOW THE BOOK *BATTLE READY* IS INSPIRING ME...

MY 3 BIG ETERNITY GOALS...

God, what are you calling me to do with my life?

one

two

three

WHAT TO DO TODAY...

God, what little steps should I take today to see these things through?

one

IDEA:

HOW I'LL DO IT:

WHEN/HOW I'LL KNOW THIS IS COMPLETE:

two

IDEA:

HOW I'LL DO IT:

WHEN/HOW I'LL KNOW THIS IS COMPLETE:

three

IDEA:

HOW I'LL DO IT:

WHEN/HOW I'LL KNOW THIS IS COMPLETE:

It is not striving that will progress you forward, but rather abiding, sitting with God, and following His heart prompts.
KELLY BALARIE, BATTLE READY

GETTING NEGATIVITY & MISTRUTHS OUTTA THE WAY...

God, what negative mental thoughts might arise as I press into these goals?

I won't let them impact my day, because I am preparing my mind to believe...

NOW I PRAY...

...AND TRUST GOD ALONG THE WAY.

What might I experience by following God's plan above, today? What fruit and life might it produce in the future?

HOW THE BOOK *BATTLE READY* IS INSPIRING ME...

MY 3 BIG ETERNITY GOALS...

God, what are you calling me to do with my life?

one

two

three

WHAT TO DO TODAY...

God, what little steps should I take today to see these things through?

one

IDEA:

HOW I'LL DO IT:

WHEN/HOW I'LL KNOW THIS IS COMPLETE:

two

IDEA:

HOW I'LL DO IT:

WHEN/HOW I'LL KNOW THIS IS COMPLETE:

three

IDEA:

HOW I'LL DO IT:

WHEN/HOW I'LL KNOW THIS IS COMPLETE:

He will wipe every tear from their eyes. There will be no more death' or mourning or crying or pain, for the old order of things has passed away.

REVELATION 21:4, NIV

GETTING NEGATIVITY & MISTRUTHS OUTTA THE WAY...

God, what negative mental thoughts might arise as I press into these goals?

I won't let them impact my day, because I am preparing my mind to believe...

NOW I PRAY...

...AND TRUST GOD ALONG THE WAY.

What might I experience by following God's plan above, today? What fruit and life might it produce in the future?

HOW THE BOOK *BATTLE READY* IS INSPIRING ME...

MY 3 BIG ETERNITY GOALS...

God, what are you calling me to do with my life?

one

two

three

WHAT TO DO TODAY...

God, what little steps should I take today to see these things through?

one

IDEA:

HOW I'LL DO IT:

WHEN/HOW I'LL KNOW THIS IS COMPLETE:

two

IDEA:

HOW I'LL DO IT:

WHEN/HOW I'LL KNOW THIS IS COMPLETE:

three

IDEA:

HOW I'LL DO IT:

WHEN/HOW I'LL KNOW THIS IS COMPLETE:

Insecurity tends to sit in the basement, all proud
it isn't sinning or making a fool of itself.
KELLY BALARIE, BATTLE READY

GETTING NEGATIVITY & MISTRUTHS OUTTA THE WAY...

God, what negative mental thoughts might arise as I press into these goals?

I won't let them impact my day, because I am preparing my mind to believe...

NOW I PRAY...

...AND TRUST GOD ALONG THE WAY.

What might I experience by following God's plan above, today? What fruit and life might it produce in the future?

HOW THE BOOK *BATTLE READY* IS INSPIRING ME...

MY 3 BIG ETERNITY GOALS...

God, what are you calling me to do with my life?

one

two

three

WHAT TO DO TODAY...

God, what little steps should I take today to see these things through?

one

IDEA:

HOW I'LL DO IT:

WHEN/HOW I'LL KNOW THIS IS COMPLETE:

two

IDEA:

HOW I'LL DO IT:

WHEN/HOW I'LL KNOW THIS IS COMPLETE:

three

IDEA:

HOW I'LL DO IT:

WHEN/HOW I'LL KNOW THIS IS COMPLETE:

Those who hope in the LORD will renew their strength. They will soar on wings like eagles; they will run and not grow weary, they will walk and not be faint.

ISAIAH 40:31, NIV

GETTING NEGATIVITY & MISTRUTHS OUTTA THE WAY...

God, what negative mental thoughts might arise as I press into these goals?

I won't let them impact my day, because I am preparing my mind to believe...

NOW I PRAY...

...AND TRUST GOD ALONG THE WAY.

What might I experience by following God's plan above, today? What fruit and life might it produce in the future?

HOW THE BOOK *BATTLE READY* IS INSPIRING ME...

MY 3 BIG ETERNITY GOALS...

God, what are you calling me to do with my life?

one

two

three

WHAT TO DO TODAY...

God, what little steps should I take today to see these things through?

one

IDEA:

HOW I'LL DO IT:

WHEN/HOW I'LL KNOW THIS IS COMPLETE:

two

IDEA:

HOW I'LL DO IT:

WHEN/HOW I'LL KNOW THIS IS COMPLETE:

three

IDEA:

HOW I'LL DO IT:

WHEN/HOW I'LL KNOW THIS IS COMPLETE:

GETTING NEGATIVITY & MISTRUTHS OUTTA THE WAY...

God, what negative mental thoughts might arise as I press into these goals?

I won't let them impact my day, because I am preparing my mind to believe...

NOW I PRAY...

...AND TRUST GOD ALONG THE WAY.

What might I experience by following God's plan above, today? What fruit and life might it produce in the future?

HOW THE BOOK *BATTLE READY* IS INSPIRING ME...

MY 3 BIG ETERNITY GOALS...

God, what are you calling me to do with my life?

one

two

three

WHAT TO DO TODAY...

God, what little steps should I take today to see these things through?

one

IDEA:

HOW I'LL DO IT:

WHEN/HOW I'LL KNOW THIS IS COMPLETE:

two

IDEA:

HOW I'LL DO IT:

WHEN/HOW I'LL KNOW THIS IS COMPLETE:

three

IDEA:

HOW I'LL DO IT:

WHEN/HOW I'LL KNOW THIS IS COMPLETE:

I have told you these things, so that in me you may have peace. In this world you will have trouble. But take heart! I have overcome the world.

JOHN 16:33, NIV

GETTING NEGATIVITY & MISTRUTHS OUTTA THE WAY...

God, what negative mental thoughts might arise as I press into these goals?

I won't let them impact my day, because I am preparing my mind to believe...

NOW I PRAY...

...AND TRUST GOD ALONG THE WAY.

What might I experience by following God's plan above, today? What fruit and life might it produce in the future?

HOW THE BOOK *BATTLE READY* IS INSPIRING ME...

MY 3 BIG ETERNITY GOALS...

God, what are you calling me to do with my life?

one

two

three

WHAT TO DO TODAY...

God, what little steps should I take today to see these things through?

one

IDEA:

HOW I'LL DO IT:

WHEN/HOW I'LL KNOW THIS IS COMPLETE:

two

IDEA:

HOW I'LL DO IT:

WHEN/HOW I'LL KNOW THIS IS COMPLETE:

three

IDEA:

HOW I'LL DO IT:

WHEN/HOW I'LL KNOW THIS IS COMPLETE:

You see the countless reasons why you're bound to fail,
God sees the infinite reasons why He can do anything.
KELLY BALARIE, BATTLE READY

GETTING NEGATIVITY & MISTRUTHS OUTTA THE WAY...

God, what negative mental thoughts might arise as I press into these goals?

I won't let them impact my day, because I am preparing my mind to believe...

NOW I PRAY...

...AND TRUST GOD ALONG THE WAY.

What might I experience by following God's plan above, today? What fruit and life might it produce in the future?

HOW THE BOOK *BATTLE READY* IS INSPIRING ME...

MY 3 BIG ETERNITY GOALS...

God, what are you calling me to do with my life?

one

two

three

WHAT TO DO TODAY...

God, what little steps should I take today to see these things through?

one

IDEA:

HOW I'LL DO IT:

WHEN/HOW I'LL KNOW THIS IS COMPLETE:

two

IDEA:

HOW I'LL DO IT:

WHEN/HOW I'LL KNOW THIS IS COMPLETE:

three

IDEA:

HOW I'LL DO IT:

WHEN/HOW I'LL KNOW THIS IS COMPLETE:

> *One of you routs a thousand, because the LORD*
> *your God fights for you, just as he promised.*
> **JOSHUA 23:10, NIV**

GETTING NEGATIVITY & MISTRUTHS OUTTA THE WAY...

God, what negative mental thoughts might arise as I press into these goals?

I won't let them impact my day, because I am preparing my mind to believe...

NOW I PRAY...

...AND TRUST GOD ALONG THE WAY.

What might I experience by following God's plan above, today? What fruit and life might it produce in the future?

HOW THE BOOK *BATTLE READY* IS INSPIRING ME...

MY 3 BIG ETERNITY GOALS...

God, what are you calling me to do with my life?

one

two

three

WHAT TO DO TODAY...

God, what little steps should I take today to see these things through?

one

IDEA:

HOW I'LL DO IT:

WHEN/HOW I'LL KNOW THIS IS COMPLETE:

two

IDEA:

HOW I'LL DO IT:

WHEN/HOW I'LL KNOW THIS IS COMPLETE:

three

IDEA:

HOW I'LL DO IT:

WHEN/HOW I'LL KNOW THIS IS COMPLETE:

We fail to mind our mind.
KELLY BALARIE, BATTLE READY

GETTING NEGATIVITY & MISTRUTHS OUTTA THE WAY...

God, what negative mental thoughts might arise as I press into these goals?

I won't let them impact my day, because I am preparing my mind to believe...

NOW I PRAY...

...AND TRUST GOD ALONG THE WAY.

What might I experience by following God's plan above, today? What fruit and life might it produce in the future?

HOW THE BOOK *BATTLE READY* IS INSPIRING ME...

MY 3 BIG ETERNITY GOALS...

God, what are you calling me to do with my life?

one

two

three

WHAT TO DO TODAY...

God, what little steps should I take today to see these things through?

one

IDEA:

HOW I'LL DO IT:

WHEN/HOW I'LL KNOW THIS IS COMPLETE:

two

IDEA:

HOW I'LL DO IT:

WHEN/HOW I'LL KNOW THIS IS COMPLETE:

three

IDEA:

HOW I'LL DO IT:

WHEN/HOW I'LL KNOW THIS IS COMPLETE:

Through you we push back our enemies;
through your name we trample our foes.
PSALM 44:5, NIV

GETTING NEGATIVITY & MISTRUTHS OUTTA THE WAY...

God, what negative mental thoughts might arise as I press into these goals?

I won't let them impact my day, because I am preparing my mind to believe...

NOW I PRAY...

...AND TRUST GOD ALONG THE WAY.

What might I experience by following God's plan above, today? What fruit and life might it produce in the future?

HOW THE BOOK *BATTLE READY* IS INSPIRING ME...

MY 3 BIG ETERNITY GOALS...

God, what are you calling me to do with my life?

one

two

three

WHAT TO DO TODAY...

God, what little steps should I take today to see these things through?

one

IDEA:

HOW I'LL DO IT:

WHEN/HOW I'LL KNOW THIS IS COMPLETE:

two

IDEA:

HOW I'LL DO IT:

WHEN/HOW I'LL KNOW THIS IS COMPLETE:

three

IDEA:

HOW I'LL DO IT:

WHEN/HOW I'LL KNOW THIS IS COMPLETE:

GETTING NEGATIVITY & MISTRUTHS OUTTA THE WAY...

God, what negative mental thoughts might arise as I press into these goals?

I won't let them impact my day, because I am preparing my mind to believe...

NOW I PRAY...

...AND TRUST GOD ALONG THE WAY.

What might I experience by following God's plan above, today? What fruit and life might it produce in the future?

HOW THE BOOK *BATTLE READY* IS INSPIRING ME...

MY 3 BIG ETERNITY GOALS...

God, what are you calling me to do with my life?

one

two

three

WHAT TO DO TODAY...

God, what little steps should I take today to see these things through?

one

IDEA:

HOW I'LL DO IT:

WHEN/HOW I'LL KNOW THIS IS COMPLETE:

two

IDEA:

HOW I'LL DO IT:

WHEN/HOW I'LL KNOW THIS IS COMPLETE:

three

IDEA:

HOW I'LL DO IT:

WHEN/HOW I'LL KNOW THIS IS COMPLETE:

The Lord will cause your enemies who rise against you to be defeated before you.
They shall come out against you one way and flee before you seven ways.
DEUTERONOMY 28:7, NIV

GETTING NEGATIVITY & MISTRUTHS OUTTA THE WAY...

God, what negative mental thoughts might arise as I press into these goals?

I won't let them impact my day, because I am preparing my mind to believe...

NOW I PRAY...

...AND TRUST GOD ALONG THE WAY.

What might I experience by following God's plan above, today? What fruit and life might it produce in the future?

HOW THE BOOK *BATTLE READY* IS INSPIRING ME...

MY 3 BIG ETERNITY GOALS...

God, what are you calling me to do with my life?

one

two

three

WHAT TO DO TODAY...

God, what little steps should I take today to see these things through?

one

IDEA:

HOW I'LL DO IT:

WHEN/HOW I'LL KNOW THIS IS COMPLETE:

two

IDEA:

HOW I'LL DO IT:

WHEN/HOW I'LL KNOW THIS IS COMPLETE:

three

IDEA:

HOW I'LL DO IT:

WHEN/HOW I'LL KNOW THIS IS COMPLETE:

GETTING NEGATIVITY & MISTRUTHS OUTTA THE WAY...

God, what negative mental thoughts might arise as I press into these goals?

I won't let them impact my day, because I am preparing my mind to believe...

NOW I PRAY...

...AND TRUST GOD ALONG THE WAY.

What might I experience by following God's plan above, today? What fruit and life might it produce in the future?

HOW THE BOOK *BATTLE READY* IS INSPIRING ME...

MY 3 BIG ETERNITY GOALS...

God, what are you calling me to do with my life?

one

two

three

WHAT TO DO TODAY...

God, what little steps should I take today to see these things through?

one

IDEA:

HOW I'LL DO IT:

WHEN/HOW I'LL KNOW THIS IS COMPLETE:

two

IDEA:

HOW I'LL DO IT:

WHEN/HOW I'LL KNOW THIS IS COMPLETE:

three

IDEA:

HOW I'LL DO IT:

WHEN/HOW I'LL KNOW THIS IS COMPLETE:

GETTING NEGATIVITY & MISTRUTHS OUTTA THE WAY...

God, what negative mental thoughts might arise as I press into these goals?

I won't let them impact my day, because I am preparing my mind to believe...

NOW I PRAY...

...AND TRUST GOD ALONG THE WAY.

What might I experience by following God's plan above, today? What fruit and life might it produce in the future?

HOW THE BOOK *BATTLE READY* IS INSPIRING ME...

MY 3 BIG ETERNITY GOALS...

God, what are you calling me to do with my life?

one

two

three

WHAT TO DO TODAY...

God, what little steps should I take today to see these things through?

one

IDEA:

HOW I'LL DO IT:

WHEN/HOW I'LL KNOW THIS IS COMPLETE:

two

IDEA:

HOW I'LL DO IT:

WHEN/HOW I'LL KNOW THIS IS COMPLETE:

three

IDEA:

HOW I'LL DO IT:

WHEN/HOW I'LL KNOW THIS IS COMPLETE:

God's truth not grasped in a heart never works. It drops dead.
KELLY BALARIE, BATTLE READY

GETTING NEGATIVITY & MISTRUTHS OUTTA THE WAY...

God, what negative mental thoughts might arise as I press into these goals?

I won't let them impact my day, because I am preparing my mind to believe...

NOW I PRAY...

...AND TRUST GOD ALONG THE WAY.

What might I experience by following God's plan above, today? What fruit and life might it produce in the future?

HOW THE BOOK *BATTLE READY* IS INSPIRING ME...

MY 3 BIG ETERNITY GOALS...

God, what are you calling me to do with my life?

one

two

three

WHAT TO DO TODAY...

God, what little steps should I take today to see these things through?

one

IDEA:

HOW I'LL DO IT:

WHEN/HOW I'LL KNOW THIS IS COMPLETE:

two

IDEA:

HOW I'LL DO IT:

WHEN/HOW I'LL KNOW THIS IS COMPLETE:

three

IDEA:

HOW I'LL DO IT:

WHEN/HOW I'LL KNOW THIS IS COMPLETE:

GETTING NEGATIVITY & MISTRUTHS OUTTA THE WAY...

God, what negative mental thoughts might arise as I press into these goals?

I won't let them impact my day, because I am preparing my mind to believe...

NOW I PRAY...

...AND TRUST GOD ALONG THE WAY.

What might I experience by following God's plan above, today? What fruit and life might it produce in the future?

HOW THE BOOK *BATTLE READY* IS INSPIRING ME...

MY 3 BIG ETERNITY GOALS...

God, what are you calling me to do with my life?

one

two

three

WHAT TO DO TODAY...

God, what little steps should I take today to see these things through?

one

IDEA:

HOW I'LL DO IT:

WHEN/HOW I'LL KNOW THIS IS COMPLETE:

two

IDEA:

HOW I'LL DO IT:

WHEN/HOW I'LL KNOW THIS IS COMPLETE:

three

IDEA:

HOW I'LL DO IT:

WHEN/HOW I'LL KNOW THIS IS COMPLETE:

Starting anything is half the battle.
KELLY BALARIE, BATTLE READY

GETTING NEGATIVITY & MISTRUTHS OUTTA THE WAY...

God, what negative mental thoughts might arise as I press into these goals?

I won't let them impact my day, because I am preparing my mind to believe...

NOW I PRAY...

...AND TRUST GOD ALONG THE WAY.

What might I experience by following God's plan above, today? What fruit and life might it produce in the future?

HOW THE BOOK *BATTLE READY* IS INSPIRING ME...

MY 3 BIG ETERNITY GOALS...

God, what are you calling me to do with my life?

one

two

three

WHAT TO DO TODAY...

God, what little steps should I take today to see these things through?

one

IDEA:

HOW I'LL DO IT:

WHEN/HOW I'LL KNOW THIS IS COMPLETE:

two

IDEA:

HOW I'LL DO IT:

WHEN/HOW I'LL KNOW THIS IS COMPLETE:

three

IDEA:

HOW I'LL DO IT:

WHEN/HOW I'LL KNOW THIS IS COMPLETE:

GETTING NEGATIVITY & MISTRUTHS OUTTA THE WAY...

God, what negative mental thoughts might arise as I press into these goals?

I won't let them impact my day, because I am preparing my mind to believe...

NOW I PRAY...

...AND TRUST GOD ALONG THE WAY.

What might I experience by following God's plan above, today? What fruit and life might it produce in the future?

HOW THE BOOK *BATTLE READY* IS INSPIRING ME...

MY 3 BIG ETERNITY GOALS...

God, what are you calling me to do with my life?

one

two

three

WHAT TO DO TODAY...

God, what little steps should I take today to see these things through?

one

IDEA:

HOW I'LL DO IT:

WHEN/HOW I'LL KNOW THIS IS COMPLETE:

two

IDEA:

HOW I'LL DO IT:

WHEN/HOW I'LL KNOW THIS IS COMPLETE:

three

IDEA:

HOW I'LL DO IT:

WHEN/HOW I'LL KNOW THIS IS COMPLETE:

Spirit-in-us, because he loves us, doesn't let us easily get away with stuff that wants to hurt us.
KELLY BALARIE, BATTLE READY

GETTING NEGATIVITY & MISTRUTHS OUTTA THE WAY...

God, what negative mental thoughts might arise as I press into these goals?

I won't let them impact my day, because I am preparing my mind to believe...

NOW I PRAY...

...AND TRUST GOD ALONG THE WAY.

What might I experience by following God's plan above, today? What fruit and life might it produce in the future?

HOW THE BOOK *BATTLE READY* IS INSPIRING ME...

MY 3 BIG ETERNITY GOALS...

God, what are you calling me to do with my life?

one

two

three

WHAT TO DO TODAY...

God, what little steps should I take today to see these things through?

one

IDEA:

HOW I'LL DO IT:

WHEN/HOW I'LL KNOW THIS IS COMPLETE:

two

IDEA:

HOW I'LL DO IT:

WHEN/HOW I'LL KNOW THIS IS COMPLETE:

three

IDEA:

HOW I'LL DO IT:

WHEN/HOW I'LL KNOW THIS IS COMPLETE:

GETTING NEGATIVITY & MISTRUTHS OUTTA THE WAY...

God, what negative mental thoughts might arise as I press into these goals?

I won't let them impact my day, because I am preparing my mind to believe...

NOW I PRAY...

...AND TRUST GOD ALONG THE WAY.

What might I experience by following God's plan above, today? What fruit and life might it produce in the future?

HOW THE BOOK *BATTLE READY* IS INSPIRING ME...

MY 3 BIG ETERNITY GOALS...

God, what are you calling me to do with my life?

one

two

three

WHAT TO DO TODAY...

God, what little steps should I take today to see these things through?

one

IDEA:

HOW I'LL DO IT:

WHEN/HOW I'LL KNOW THIS IS COMPLETE:

two

IDEA:

HOW I'LL DO IT:

WHEN/HOW I'LL KNOW THIS IS COMPLETE:

three

IDEA:

HOW I'LL DO IT:

WHEN/HOW I'LL KNOW THIS IS COMPLETE:

GETTING NEGATIVITY & MISTRUTHS OUTTA THE WAY...

God, what negative mental thoughts might arise as I press into these goals?

I won't let them impact my day, because I am preparing my mind to believe...

NOW I PRAY...

...AND TRUST GOD ALONG THE WAY.

What might I experience by following God's plan above, today? What fruit and life might it produce in the future?

HOW THE BOOK *BATTLE READY* IS INSPIRING ME...

MY 3 BIG ETERNITY GOALS...

God, what are you calling me to do with my life?

one

two

three

WHAT TO DO TODAY...

God, what little steps should I take today to see these things through?

one

IDEA:

HOW I'LL DO IT:

WHEN/HOW I'LL KNOW THIS IS COMPLETE:

two

IDEA:

HOW I'LL DO IT:

WHEN/HOW I'LL KNOW THIS IS COMPLETE:

three

IDEA:

HOW I'LL DO IT:

WHEN/HOW I'LL KNOW THIS IS COMPLETE:

Blessed be the LORD, my rock, Who trains my hands for war, And my fingers for battle.

PSALM 144:1, NIV

GETTING NEGATIVITY & MISTRUTHS OUTTA THE WAY...

God, what negative mental thoughts might arise as I press into these goals?

I won't let them impact my day, because I am preparing my mind to believe...

NOW I PRAY...

...AND TRUST GOD ALONG THE WAY.

What might I experience by following God's plan above, today? What fruit and life might it produce in the future?

HOW THE BOOK *BATTLE READY* IS INSPIRING ME...

MY 3 BIG ETERNITY GOALS...

God, what are you calling me to do with my life?

one

two

three

WHAT TO DO TODAY...

God, what little steps should I take today to see these things through?

one

IDEA:

HOW I'LL DO IT:

WHEN/HOW I'LL KNOW THIS IS COMPLETE:

two

IDEA:

HOW I'LL DO IT:

WHEN/HOW I'LL KNOW THIS IS COMPLETE:

three

IDEA:

HOW I'LL DO IT:

WHEN/HOW I'LL KNOW THIS IS COMPLETE:

Repentance ≠ Retaliation by God
Repentance = Restoration by God
KELLY BALARIE, BATTLE READY

GETTING NEGATIVITY & MISTRUTHS OUTTA THE WAY...

God, what negative mental thoughts might arise as I press into these goals?

I won't let them impact my day, because I am preparing my mind to believe...

NOW I PRAY...

...AND TRUST GOD ALONG THE WAY.

What might I experience by following God's plan above, today? What fruit and life might it produce in the future?

HOW THE BOOK *BATTLE READY* IS INSPIRING ME...

MY 3 BIG ETERNITY GOALS...

God, what are you calling me to do with my life?

one

two

three

WHAT TO DO TODAY...

God, what little steps should I take today to see these things through?

one

IDEA:

HOW I'LL DO IT:

WHEN/HOW I'LL KNOW THIS IS COMPLETE:

two

IDEA:

HOW I'LL DO IT:

WHEN/HOW I'LL KNOW THIS IS COMPLETE:

three

IDEA:

HOW I'LL DO IT:

WHEN/HOW I'LL KNOW THIS IS COMPLETE:

When I called, you answered me; you greatly emboldened me.
PSALM 138:3, NIV

GETTING NEGATIVITY & MISTRUTHS OUTTA THE WAY...

God, what negative mental thoughts might arise as I press into these goals?

I won't let them impact my day, because I am preparing my mind to believe...

NOW I PRAY...

...AND TRUST GOD ALONG THE WAY.

What might I experience by following God's plan above, today? What fruit and life might it produce in the future?

HOW THE BOOK *BATTLE READY* IS INSPIRING ME...

MY 3 BIG ETERNITY GOALS...

God, what are you calling me to do with my life?

one

two

three

WHAT TO DO TODAY...

God, what little steps should I take today to see these things through?

one

IDEA:

HOW I'LL DO IT:

WHEN/HOW I'LL KNOW THIS IS COMPLETE:

two

IDEA:

HOW I'LL DO IT:

WHEN/HOW I'LL KNOW THIS IS COMPLETE:

three

IDEA:

HOW I'LL DO IT:

WHEN/HOW I'LL KNOW THIS IS COMPLETE:

GETTING NEGATIVITY & MISTRUTHS OUTTA THE WAY...

God, what negative mental thoughts might arise as I press into these goals?

I won't let them impact my day, because I am preparing my mind to believe...

NOW I PRAY...

...AND TRUST GOD ALONG THE WAY.

What might I experience by following God's plan above, today? What fruit and life might it produce in the future?

HOW THE BOOK *BATTLE READY* IS INSPIRING ME...

MY 3 BIG ETERNITY GOALS...

God, what are you calling me to do with my life?

one

two

three

WHAT TO DO TODAY...

God, what little steps should I take today to see these things through?

one

IDEA:

HOW I'LL DO IT:

WHEN/HOW I'LL KNOW THIS IS COMPLETE:

two

IDEA:

HOW I'LL DO IT:

WHEN/HOW I'LL KNOW THIS IS COMPLETE:

three

IDEA:

HOW I'LL DO IT:

WHEN/HOW I'LL KNOW THIS IS COMPLETE:

Put on the full armor of God, so that you can take your stand against the devil's schemes.
PSALM 138:3, NIV

GETTING NEGATIVITY & MISTRUTHS OUTTA THE WAY...

God, what negative mental thoughts might arise as I press into these goals?

I won't let them impact my day, because I am preparing my mind to believe...

NOW I PRAY...

...AND TRUST GOD ALONG THE WAY.

What might I experience by following God's plan above, today? What fruit and life might it produce in the future?

HOW THE BOOK *BATTLE READY* IS INSPIRING ME...

MY 3 BIG ETERNITY GOALS...

God, what are you calling me to do with my life?

one
two
three

WHAT TO DO TODAY...

God, what little steps should I take today to see these things through?

one

IDEA:

HOW I'LL DO IT:

WHEN/HOW I'LL KNOW THIS IS COMPLETE:

two

IDEA:

HOW I'LL DO IT:

WHEN/HOW I'LL KNOW THIS IS COMPLETE:

three

IDEA:

HOW I'LL DO IT:

WHEN/HOW I'LL KNOW THIS IS COMPLETE:

GETTING NEGATIVITY & MISTRUTHS OUTTA THE WAY...

God, what negative mental thoughts might arise as I press into these goals?

I won't let them impact my day, because I am preparing my mind to believe...

NOW I PRAY...

...AND TRUST GOD ALONG THE WAY.

What might I experience by following God's plan above, today? What fruit and life might it produce in the future?

HOW THE BOOK *BATTLE READY* IS INSPIRING ME...

MY 3 BIG ETERNITY GOALS...

God, what are you calling me to do with my life?

one

two

three

WHAT TO DO TODAY...

God, what little steps should I take today to see these things through?

one

IDEA:

HOW I'LL DO IT:

WHEN/HOW I'LL KNOW THIS IS COMPLETE:

two

IDEA:

HOW I'LL DO IT:

WHEN/HOW I'LL KNOW THIS IS COMPLETE:

three

IDEA:

HOW I'LL DO IT:

WHEN/HOW I'LL KNOW THIS IS COMPLETE:

GETTING NEGATIVITY & MISTRUTHS OUTTA THE WAY...

God, what negative mental thoughts might arise as I press into these goals?

I won't let them impact my day, because I am preparing my mind to believe...

NOW I PRAY...

...AND TRUST GOD ALONG THE WAY.

What might I experience by following God's plan above, today? What fruit and life might it produce in the future?

HOW THE BOOK *BATTLE READY* IS INSPIRING ME...

MY 3 BIG ETERNITY GOALS...

God, what are you calling me to do with my life?

one

two

three

WHAT TO DO TODAY...

God, what little steps should I take today to see these things through?

one

IDEA:

HOW I'LL DO IT:

WHEN/HOW I'LL KNOW THIS IS COMPLETE:

two

IDEA:

HOW I'LL DO IT:

WHEN/HOW I'LL KNOW THIS IS COMPLETE:

three

IDEA:

HOW I'LL DO IT:

WHEN/HOW I'LL KNOW THIS IS COMPLETE:

The Spirit gives us God's inside view, so we don't have to rely on our own.
KELLY BALARIE, BATTLE READY

GETTING NEGATIVITY & MISTRUTHS OUTTA THE WAY...

God, what negative mental thoughts might arise as I press into these goals?

I won't let them impact my day, because I am preparing my mind to believe...

NOW I PRAY...

...AND TRUST GOD ALONG THE WAY.

What might I experience by following God's plan above, today? What fruit and life might it produce in the future?

HOW THE BOOK *BATTLE READY* IS INSPIRING ME...

MY 3 BIG ETERNITY GOALS...

God, what are you calling me to do with my life?

one

two

three

WHAT TO DO TODAY...

God, what little steps should I take today to see these things through?

one

IDEA:

HOW I'LL DO IT:

WHEN/HOW I'LL KNOW THIS IS COMPLETE:

two

IDEA:

HOW I'LL DO IT:

WHEN/HOW I'LL KNOW THIS IS COMPLETE:

three

IDEA:

HOW I'LL DO IT:

WHEN/HOW I'LL KNOW THIS IS COMPLETE:

> *What, then, shall we say in response to these things?*
> *If God is for us, who can be against us?*
> 1 CORINTHIANS 15:57, NIV

GETTING NEGATIVITY & MISTRUTHS OUTTA THE WAY...

God, what negative mental thoughts might arise as I press into these goals?

I won't let them impact my day, because I am preparing my mind to believe...

NOW I PRAY...

...AND TRUST GOD ALONG THE WAY.

What might I experience by following God's plan above, today? What fruit and life might it produce in the future?

HOW THE BOOK *BATTLE READY* IS INSPIRING ME...

MY 3 BIG ETERNITY GOALS...

God, what are you calling me to do with my life?

one

two

three

WHAT TO DO TODAY...

God, what little steps should I take today to see these things through?

one

IDEA:

HOW I'LL DO IT:

WHEN/HOW I'LL KNOW THIS IS COMPLETE:

two

IDEA:

HOW I'LL DO IT:

WHEN/HOW I'LL KNOW THIS IS COMPLETE:

three

IDEA:

HOW I'LL DO IT:

WHEN/HOW I'LL KNOW THIS IS COMPLETE:

GETTING NEGATIVITY & MISTRUTHS OUTTA THE WAY...

God, what negative mental thoughts might arise as I press into these goals?

I won't let them impact my day, because I am preparing my mind to believe...

NOW I PRAY...

...AND TRUST GOD ALONG THE WAY.

What might I experience by following God's plan above, today? What fruit and life might it produce in the future?

HOW THE BOOK *BATTLE READY* IS INSPIRING ME...

MY 3 BIG ETERNITY GOALS...

God, what are you calling me to do with my life?

one

two

three

WHAT TO DO TODAY...

God, what little steps should I take today to see these things through?

one

IDEA:

HOW I'LL DO IT:

WHEN/HOW I'LL KNOW THIS IS COMPLETE:

two

IDEA:

HOW I'LL DO IT:

WHEN/HOW I'LL KNOW THIS IS COMPLETE:

three

IDEA:

HOW I'LL DO IT:

WHEN/HOW I'LL KNOW THIS IS COMPLETE:

The LORD is my strength and my shield; My heart trusts in Him, and I am helped; Therefore my heart exults, And with my song I shall thank Him.
PSALM 28:7, NIV

GETTING NEGATIVITY & MISTRUTHS OUTTA THE WAY...

God, what negative mental thoughts might arise as I press into these goals?

I won't let them impact my day, because I am preparing my mind to believe...

NOW I PRAY...

...AND TRUST GOD ALONG THE WAY.

What might I experience by following God's plan above, today? What fruit and life might it produce in the future?

HOW THE BOOK *BATTLE READY* IS INSPIRING ME...

MY 3 BIG ETERNITY GOALS...

God, what are you calling me to do with my life?

one

two

three

WHAT TO DO TODAY...

God, what little steps should I take today to see these things through?

one

IDEA:

HOW I'LL DO IT:

WHEN/HOW I'LL KNOW THIS IS COMPLETE:

two

IDEA:

HOW I'LL DO IT:

WHEN/HOW I'LL KNOW THIS IS COMPLETE:

three

IDEA:

HOW I'LL DO IT:

WHEN/HOW I'LL KNOW THIS IS COMPLETE:

GETTING NEGATIVITY & MISTRUTHS OUTTA THE WAY...

God, what negative mental thoughts might arise as I press into these goals?

I won't let them impact my day, because I am preparing my mind to believe...

NOW I PRAY...

...AND TRUST GOD ALONG THE WAY.

What might I experience by following God's plan above, today? What fruit and life might it produce in the future?

HOW THE BOOK *BATTLE READY* IS INSPIRING ME...

MY 3 BIG ETERNITY GOALS...

God, what are you calling me to do with my life?

one
two
three

WHAT TO DO TODAY...

God, what little steps should I take today to see these things through?

one
IDEA:

HOW I'LL DO IT:

WHEN/HOW I'LL KNOW THIS IS COMPLETE:

two
IDEA:

HOW I'LL DO IT:

WHEN/HOW I'LL KNOW THIS IS COMPLETE:

three
IDEA:

HOW I'LL DO IT:

WHEN/HOW I'LL KNOW THIS IS COMPLETE:

> *Therefore, with minds that are alert and fully sober, set your hope on the grace to be brought to you when Jesus Christ is revealed at his coming.*
> **1 PETER 1:13, NIV**

GETTING NEGATIVITY & MISTRUTHS OUTTA THE WAY...

God, what negative mental thoughts might arise as I press into these goals?

I won't let them impact my day, because I am preparing my mind to believe...

NOW I PRAY...

...AND TRUST GOD ALONG THE WAY.

What might I experience by following God's plan above, today? What fruit and life might it produce in the future?

HOW THE BOOK *BATTLE READY* IS INSPIRING ME...

MY 3 BIG ETERNITY GOALS...

God, what are you calling me to do with my life?

one

two

three

WHAT TO DO TODAY...

God, what little steps should I take today to see these things through?

one

IDEA:

HOW I'LL DO IT:

WHEN/HOW I'LL KNOW THIS IS COMPLETE:

two

IDEA:

HOW I'LL DO IT:

WHEN/HOW I'LL KNOW THIS IS COMPLETE:

three

IDEA:

HOW I'LL DO IT:

WHEN/HOW I'LL KNOW THIS IS COMPLETE:

GETTING NEGATIVITY & MISTRUTHS OUTTA THE WAY...

God, what negative mental thoughts might arise as I press into these goals?

I won't let them impact my day, because I am preparing my mind to believe...

NOW I PRAY...

...AND TRUST GOD ALONG THE WAY.

What might I experience by following God's plan above, today? What fruit and life might it produce in the future?

HOW THE BOOK *BATTLE READY* IS INSPIRING ME...

MY 3 BIG ETERNITY GOALS...

God, what are you calling me to do with my life?

one

two

three

WHAT TO DO TODAY...

God, what little steps should I take today to see these things through?

one

IDEA:

HOW I'LL DO IT:

WHEN/HOW I'LL KNOW THIS IS COMPLETE:

two

IDEA:

HOW I'LL DO IT:

WHEN/HOW I'LL KNOW THIS IS COMPLETE:

three

IDEA:

HOW I'LL DO IT:

WHEN/HOW I'LL KNOW THIS IS COMPLETE:

GETTING NEGATIVITY & MISTRUTHS OUTTA THE WAY...

God, what negative mental thoughts might arise as I press into these goals?

I won't let them impact my day, because I am preparing my mind to believe...

NOW I PRAY...

...AND TRUST GOD ALONG THE WAY.

What might I experience by following God's plan above, today? What fruit and life might it produce in the future?

HOW THE BOOK *BATTLE READY* IS INSPIRING ME...

MY 3 BIG ETERNITY GOALS...

God, what are you calling me to do with my life?

one

two

three

WHAT TO DO TODAY...

God, what little steps should I take today to see these things through?

one

IDEA:

HOW I'LL DO IT:

WHEN/HOW I'LL KNOW THIS IS COMPLETE:

two

IDEA:

HOW I'LL DO IT:

WHEN/HOW I'LL KNOW THIS IS COMPLETE:

three

IDEA:

HOW I'LL DO IT:

WHEN/HOW I'LL KNOW THIS IS COMPLETE:

GETTING NEGATIVITY & MISTRUTHS OUTTA THE WAY...

God, what negative mental thoughts might arise as I press into these goals?

I won't let them impact my day, because I am preparing my mind to believe...

NOW I PRAY...

...AND TRUST GOD ALONG THE WAY.

What might I experience by following God's plan above, today? What fruit and life might it produce in the future?

HOW THE BOOK *BATTLE READY* IS INSPIRING ME...

MY 3 BIG ETERNITY GOALS...

God, what are you calling me to do with my life?

one

two

three

WHAT TO DO TODAY...

God, what little steps should I take today to see these things through?

one

IDEA:

HOW I'LL DO IT:

WHEN/HOW I'LL KNOW THIS IS COMPLETE:

two

IDEA:

HOW I'LL DO IT:

WHEN/HOW I'LL KNOW THIS IS COMPLETE:

three

IDEA:

HOW I'LL DO IT:

WHEN/HOW I'LL KNOW THIS IS COMPLETE:

> *Be strong and courageous. Do not be afraid or terrified because of them,*
> *for the LORD your God goes with you; he will never leave you nor forsake you.*
> DEUTERONOMY 31:6, NIV

GETTING NEGATIVITY & MISTRUTHS OUTTA THE WAY...

God, what negative mental thoughts might arise as I press into these goals?

I won't let them impact my day, because I am preparing my mind to believe...

NOW I PRAY...

...AND TRUST GOD ALONG THE WAY.

What might I experience by following God's plan above, today? What fruit and life might it produce in the future?

HOW THE BOOK *BATTLE READY* IS INSPIRING ME...

MY 3 BIG ETERNITY GOALS...

God, what are you calling me to do with my life?

one

two

three

WHAT TO DO TODAY...

God, what little steps should I take today to see these things through?

one

IDEA:

HOW I'LL DO IT:

WHEN/HOW I'LL KNOW THIS IS COMPLETE:

two

IDEA:

HOW I'LL DO IT:

WHEN/HOW I'LL KNOW THIS IS COMPLETE:

three

IDEA:

HOW I'LL DO IT:

WHEN/HOW I'LL KNOW THIS IS COMPLETE:

I am able to stand on the promises of God, no matter how I feel.
KELLY BALARIE, BATTLE READY

GETTING NEGATIVITY & MISTRUTHS OUTTA THE WAY...

God, what negative mental thoughts might arise as I press into these goals?

I won't let them impact my day, because I am preparing my mind to believe...

NOW I PRAY...

...AND TRUST GOD ALONG THE WAY.

What might I experience by following God's plan above, today? What fruit and life might it produce in the future?

HOW THE BOOK *BATTLE READY* IS INSPIRING ME...

MY 3 BIG ETERNITY GOALS...

God, what are you calling me to do with my life?

one

two

three

WHAT TO DO TODAY...

God, what little steps should I take today to see these things through?

one

IDEA:

HOW I'LL DO IT:

WHEN/HOW I'LL KNOW THIS IS COMPLETE:

two

IDEA:

HOW I'LL DO IT:

WHEN/HOW I'LL KNOW THIS IS COMPLETE:

three

IDEA:

HOW I'LL DO IT:

WHEN/HOW I'LL KNOW THIS IS COMPLETE:

The thief comes only to steal and kill and destroy;
I have come that they may have life, and have it to the full.
JOHN 10:10, NIV

GETTING NEGATIVITY & MISTRUTHS OUTTA THE WAY...

God, what negative mental thoughts might arise as I press into these goals?

I won't let them impact my day, because I am preparing my mind to believe...

NOW I PRAY...

...AND TRUST GOD ALONG THE WAY.

What might I experience by following God's plan above, today? What fruit and life might it produce in the future?

HOW THE BOOK *BATTLE READY* IS INSPIRING ME...

MY 3 BIG ETERNITY GOALS...

God, what are you calling me to do with my life?

one

two

three

WHAT TO DO TODAY...

God, what little steps should I take today to see these things through?

one

IDEA:

HOW I'LL DO IT:

WHEN/HOW I'LL KNOW THIS IS COMPLETE:

two

IDEA:

HOW I'LL DO IT:

WHEN/HOW I'LL KNOW THIS IS COMPLETE:

three

IDEA:

HOW I'LL DO IT:

WHEN/HOW I'LL KNOW THIS IS COMPLETE:

GETTING NEGATIVITY & MISTRUTHS OUTTA THE WAY...

God, what negative mental thoughts might arise as I press into these goals?

I won't let them impact my day, because I am preparing my mind to believe...

NOW I PRAY...

...AND TRUST GOD ALONG THE WAY.

What might I experience by following God's plan above, today? What fruit and life might it produce in the future?

HOW THE BOOK *BATTLE READY* IS INSPIRING ME...

MY 3 BIG ETERNITY GOALS...

God, what are you calling me to do with my life?

one

two

three

WHAT TO DO TODAY...

God, what little steps should I take today to see these things through?

one

IDEA:

HOW I'LL DO IT:

WHEN/HOW I'LL KNOW THIS IS COMPLETE:

two

IDEA:

HOW I'LL DO IT:

WHEN/HOW I'LL KNOW THIS IS COMPLETE:

three

IDEA:

HOW I'LL DO IT:

WHEN/HOW I'LL KNOW THIS IS COMPLETE:

Trust in the LORD with all your heart and do not lean on your own understanding.
In all your ways acknowledge Him, and He will make your paths straight.

PROVERBS 3:5-6

GETTING NEGATIVITY & MISTRUTHS OUTTA THE WAY...

God, what negative mental thoughts might arise as I press into these goals?

I won't let them impact my day, because I am preparing my mind to believe...

NOW I PRAY...

...AND TRUST GOD ALONG THE WAY.

What might I experience by following God's plan above, today? What fruit and life might it produce in the future?

HOW THE BOOK *BATTLE READY* IS INSPIRING ME...

MY 3 BIG ETERNITY GOALS...

God, what are you calling me to do with my life?

one

two

three

WHAT TO DO TODAY...

God, what little steps should I take today to see these things through?

one

IDEA:

HOW I'LL DO IT:

WHEN/HOW I'LL KNOW THIS IS COMPLETE:

two

IDEA:

HOW I'LL DO IT:

WHEN/HOW I'LL KNOW THIS IS COMPLETE:

three

IDEA:

HOW I'LL DO IT:

WHEN/HOW I'LL KNOW THIS IS COMPLETE:

GETTING NEGATIVITY & MISTRUTHS OUTTA THE WAY...

God, what negative mental thoughts might arise as I press into these goals?

I won't let them impact my day, because I am preparing my mind to believe...

NOW I PRAY...

...AND TRUST GOD ALONG THE WAY.

What might I experience by following God's plan above, today? What fruit and life might it produce in the future?

HOW THE BOOK *BATTLE READY* IS INSPIRING ME...

MY 3 BIG ETERNITY GOALS...

God, what are you calling me to do with my life?

one

two

three

WHAT TO DO TODAY...

God, what little steps should I take today to see these things through?

one

IDEA:

HOW I'LL DO IT:

WHEN/HOW I'LL KNOW THIS IS COMPLETE:

two

IDEA:

HOW I'LL DO IT:

WHEN/HOW I'LL KNOW THIS IS COMPLETE:

three

IDEA:

HOW I'LL DO IT:

WHEN/HOW I'LL KNOW THIS IS COMPLETE:

Be strong, and let us fight bravely for our people and the cities of our God. The LORD will do what is good in his sight.

2 SAMUEL 10:12, NIV

GETTING NEGATIVITY & MISTRUTHS OUTTA THE WAY...

God, what negative mental thoughts might arise as I press into these goals?

I won't let them impact my day, because I am preparing my mind to believe...

NOW I PRAY...

...AND TRUST GOD ALONG THE WAY.

What might I experience by following God's plan above, today? What fruit and life might it produce in the future?

HOW THE BOOK *BATTLE READY* IS INSPIRING ME...

MY 3 BIG ETERNITY GOALS...

God, what are you calling me to do with my life?

one

two

three

WHAT TO DO TODAY...

God, what little steps should I take today to see these things through?

one

IDEA:

HOW I'LL DO IT:

WHEN/HOW I'LL KNOW THIS IS COMPLETE:

two

IDEA:

HOW I'LL DO IT:

WHEN/HOW I'LL KNOW THIS IS COMPLETE:

three

IDEA:

HOW I'LL DO IT:

WHEN/HOW I'LL KNOW THIS IS COMPLETE:

We have enough because we have God.
KELLY BALARIE, BATTLE READY

GETTING NEGATIVITY & MISTRUTHS OUTTA THE WAY...

God, what negative mental thoughts might arise as I press into these goals?

I won't let them impact my day, because I am preparing my mind to believe...

NOW I PRAY...

...AND TRUST GOD ALONG THE WAY.

What might I experience by following God's plan above, today? What fruit and life might it produce in the future?

HOW THE BOOK *BATTLE READY* IS INSPIRING ME...

MY 3 BIG ETERNITY GOALS...

God, what are you calling me to do with my life?

one

two

three

WHAT TO DO TODAY...

God, what little steps should I take today to see these things through?

one

IDEA:

HOW I'LL DO IT:

WHEN/HOW I'LL KNOW THIS IS COMPLETE:

two

IDEA:

HOW I'LL DO IT:

WHEN/HOW I'LL KNOW THIS IS COMPLETE:

three

IDEA:

HOW I'LL DO IT:

WHEN/HOW I'LL KNOW THIS IS COMPLETE:

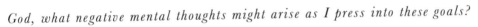

No weapon forged against you will prevail, and you will refute every tongue that accuses you. This is the heritage of the servants of the LORD, and this is their vindication from me," declares the LORD.

ISAIAH 54:17, NIV

GETTING NEGATIVITY & MISTRUTHS OUTTA THE WAY...

God, what negative mental thoughts might arise as I press into these goals?

I won't let them impact my day, because I am preparing my mind to believe...

NOW I PRAY...

...AND TRUST GOD ALONG THE WAY.

What might I experience by following God's plan above, today? What fruit and life might it produce in the future?

LOVE OTHERS WELL

Pray: **ASK GOD, HOW CAN I LOVE THESE PEOPLE WELL?**

HUSBAND:

CHILD 1:

MOM:

DAD:

SISTER:

BROTHER:

FRIEND 1:

FRIEND 2:

CO-WORKER

_____:

_____:

83579480R00113

Made in the USA
San Bernardino, CA
27 July 2018